Praise for Gary Joseph Grappo's *Get the Job You Want in Thirty Days:*

"DON'T INTERVIEW WITHOUT THIS BOOK! It's loaded with simple, straightforward advice that can make all the difference in getting the job."

> —GLORIA ROSEN KOZNESOFF, John Hancock Financial Services

"FROM WRITING THE RÉSUMÉ TO CLINCHING THE JOB, this book takes you step-by-step and tells you what to do to succeed."

> —LEON N. GRAHAM, Executive Vice President, BMG Direct

"ESSENTIAL INFORMATION . . . A GOLD MINE FOR THE JOB-SEEKER!"

> —CAROL EICHER, Director of Human Resources, The Lodge of Four Seasons

"A CLEAR, CONCISE, EASY-TO-USE BOOK NO JOB-SEEKER SHOULD BE WITHOUT."

> —STEVEN LEEK, Director of Sales Training, Edison Menswear Group

Berkley Books by Gary Joseph Grappo

GET THE JOB YOU WANT IN THIRTY DAYS
THE TOP 10 FEARS OF JOB SEEKERS

The
TOP 10
FEARS
OF JOB SEEKERS

**Your Guide to an Effective,
Stress-Free Job Search**

GARY JOSEPH GRAPPO

BERKLEY BOOKS, NEW YORK

THE TOP 10 FEARS OF JOB SEEKERS

A Berkley Book/published by arrangement with the author

PRINTING HISTORY
Berkley trade paperback edition/September 1996

The Putnam Berkley World Wide Web site address is http://www.berkley.com

ISBN: 0-425-15449-1

BERKLEY®
Berkley Books are published by The Berkley Publishing Group,
200 Madison Avenue, New York, New York 10016. BERKLEY and the "B"
design are trademarks belonging to Berkley Publishing Corporation.

PRINTED IN THE UNITED STATES OF AMERICA

10 9 8 7 6 5 4 3 2 1

Acknowledgments

A number of very important people must be recognized. Without their inspiration and help, this work could never have been created. I hold deep admiration and appreciation for Perri Capell, a senior editor at *The Wall Street Journal's National Business Employment Weekly*. It all began over lunch at The Scanticon Hotel Conference Center in Princeton, New Jersey, via her encouragement to write an article on job hunters' top fears based on my recent book tour's interaction with job seekers nationwide. The article was first published in *The Wall Street Journal's National Business Employment Weekly* on December 11, 1994, as "The Job Hunters' Top 10 Fears." Further, I am deeply grateful to my agent, Pema Browne, of Pema Browne, Ltd., and my editor at Berkley, Natalee Rosenstein, who, as a result of their undying faith in me made this book a reality. A particular thanks to John Jamieson, who was consulted for a therapist's perspective on the book's subject matter. A final note to thank John Jamieson and Timothy Kidd, who read the final draft and provided valuable feedback and suggestions.

To my sister Shelley, who inspires me and
constantly challenges me to never give up

Contents

About This Book

In *The Top 10 Fears of Job Seekers*, Gary Joseph Grappo takes your key fears and concerns about the job search process and helps you formulate solutions that start you on your way to mastering negative stress. These solutions, when understood and acted upon, will give your job search direction, power, and above all, *results*. By bringing your fears out into the light and addressing them, you will learn how to dispel these fears and eliminate the anxiety associated with them. With this straightforward advice, your success is virtually guaranteed.

In this book, you discover that many of your long-standing fears about the job search process are normal and commonly shared by most people who are job hunting. From the author's many hours of meetings with job seekers nationwide, you can now gain valuable insight into the most commonly held fears. You can overcome them and put your job quest into a power search mode.

Introduction

After the publication of *Get The Job You Want in Thirty Days*, for a brief moment it appeared as though my work in helping others was finally complete. At last, time-tested formulas were not only helping myself and close associates get jobs quickly, but through the book I was now able to expand my help to thousands of job seekers at one time. It was almost as though I was at the end of a chapter of a good book that I hated to put down. To my surprise, I discovered I was only reading the title page.

The events that followed the publication of *Get The Job You Want in Thirty Days* provided the seeds for creating this important new guide, *The Top 10 Fears of Job Seekers*. Initially, I received invitations to speak with the graduating seniors of major educational institutions such as Georgetown, Fordham, Clemson, and Penn State Universities. Next came a rigorous schedule of two-hour seminars at Barnes & Noble superstores nationwide. The turnout was tremendous. I completed numerous local and national talk shows with call-ins from around the nation.

From universities to talk shows, the message was clear: You, the job seeker, needed a professional with whom you could share your innermost fears, worries, and concerns. You needed someone who would listen and offer simple, straightforward, and savvy advice. From group to group, whether young or old, changing jobs or unemployed, job seekers have one thing in common: your top fears, worries, and concerns are the same. In most instances, however, job seekers felt unique and alone in their dilemma, and they believed that no one understood them. What I discovered was contrary to that belief. I found from group to group and from individual to individual, the fears, worries, and concerns are quite similar. That makes us all very normal. How we address our fears determines our success.

In essence, I discovered the top ten fears of job seekers after days, weeks, and months of analyzing the flip charts and taped audience feedback gathered from the seminars I taught nation-wide in conjunction with my last book. The top ten fears are based on statistical trends I discovered from these seminars. How could a twenty-six-year-old M.B.A. student in Washington, D.C., and a fifty-year-old laid-off executive in Los Angeles have the same fears? All the concerns eventually came down to some astounding commonalities.

From Los Angeles to New York, I found very qualified and tal-ented professionals, yet most were gripped by fear as a result of recent corporate downsizing. It is no surprise. In the first thirty days of 1994, American businesses laid off more than 100,000 people. Further, military spending has been cut back. This will create more layoffs as defense-related industries will lose the U.S. military's business. According to the March 8, 1993, issue of *Fortune* magazine, it has been estimated that defense-related industries alone will eliminate 2.6 million jobs over the next five years.

Many of the concerned workers I met had already been victims of downsizing. Others were still employed, but they were tense and apprehensive as the corporate ax loomed over their heads. They lived every day in fear as they wondered which one among them would be next. Their only hope was that they would be one of the few lucky ones who would somehow magically retain their job after the dust had settled. Deep in their hearts they knew luck more than likely would not be on their side. They would not have taken the time to attend my seminar otherwise.

The job market is bad. The real bad news is that it is getting worse. Why? Jackie Larson and Cheri Comstock in their book, *The New Rules of the Job Search Game*, explain that it is the result of world economics. "Large American companies are reducing the number of levels of management. For example, before a company reduces its workforce, it may have ten levels between the factory worker and the president. After downsizing, the same company has four levels between the hourly worker and the CEO. They must eliminate job divisions and departments in order to remain competitive in an increasingly global market, one without boundaries. In addition, many jobs, no longer only the unskilled ones, are going overseas where labor costs are lower."

One reason for all the fear, worry, and confusion among workers today is that they are trying to navigate troubled waters. They are asking themselves, "Why is this happening?" They are saying to themselves and to others, "I don't understand what's going on anymore."

This is a common reaction when the rules to any game have been radically changed. Imagine playing cards with a group a friends only to find out that the way you play the game is totally different than the way they play. How would you feel? Surprised? Confused? If you take the game seriously, you may even be angry. That's exactly what has happened to workers today. The rules have changed. Here are just a few examples of what has changed. This is my version of what was then and how it is now.

THEN	NOW
Companies expected long-term loyalty from employees.	Companies are satisfied with short-term (two to four years) commitment. New hires are less costly than lifers.
Work for a big company and you are set for life.	Work for a big company and get laid off.
Small companies offer few career opportunities and little growth.	According to Dun and Bradstreet, small businesses, those with fewer than 1,000 employees, comprise 90 percent of new jobs being added to the job market.

THEN	NOW
Working hard, doing your job, keeping your mouth shut, playing by the rules, and staying within your limits will guarantee you a job for life.	Be an innovator. Go beyond the rules. Don't just do your job, but be cross-utilized and do others' jobs as well. Speak up often with new ideas. Be proactive. Use it or lose it!
Job changing was considered a sign of instability.	Job changing is considered a sign of the times. Further, it is the sign of desirable employee traits such as self-confidence, high levels of self-esteem, entrepreneurism, assertiveness, drive, and ambition.
If you want security, work for a large firm that clearly dominates its share of the market.	Work for an "upstart" who, unlike a large firm, has the ability to quickly respond to market needs with new inventions and better methods. It may have its risks, but the rewards can be great.

Despite the change in rules and all the bad news you may have read about, heard, or even experienced firsthand in today's job market, letting it control our lives is not an option. It is no more an option than is staying in our homes never to leave again as a result of the news of the increasing growth in the crime rate. Overcome your fears and take control of your situation. Read on, and you'll discover exactly how to do it. You can be a winner, despite the new game and the new rules.

Tame the Psychological Lions and Tigers Within

Tricia, a national sales representative, was denied advancement and humiliated frequently by her employer, a California clothing manufacturer, before being forced out. She experienced what she terms as "no respect" from her former employer. She now fears she's not qualified for other sales jobs and that even if she does land one, a new company will treat her just as poorly. As a result, Tricia has developed the fear of working for any new employer.

Not surprisingly, Tricia has been struggling with her job search for six months. On a conscious level, she relates her inability to find a job to a lack of time, contacts, access to a computer, and other rationalizations. She knows, however, that her underlying fears are the real reason for her job-search paralysis.

Being unemployed or making a career change can be scary. Unlike prehistoric times, when cave dwellers fled from wild animals, job hunters today have psychological lions and tigers to tame. Low self-esteem, feelings of worthlessness, and depression, are some examples of these modern-day threats. These fears threaten job seekers' well-being and prevent them from reaching their goals.

Fear puts our quest for success in reverse. As a result, we shield ourselves from rejection, make fewer contacts, and avoid result-oriented activities. Ironically, although finding a new position is your primary goal, negative body language, images, and statements will project an overall message that says, "Don't hire me!" The results of fear range from an inability to network and make contacts, to being unable to sell oneself effectively when even the most casual contact would have helped create a job offer.

Before we get overwhelmed by all our fears, let's put them into proper perspective. A certain amount of fear exists in everyone. Without it, how would we know to jump back off the curb when we see a truck heading our way too close for comfort on a rainy day? How would we know that it is time to improve our eating habits as a result of a recent physical exam that revealed our cholesterol was too high?

Fear in many instances is constructive and beneficial. Over the years, I have worked for companies that have either gone bankrupt or had been taken over. I was out of a job more times than I care to remember. Was I fearful in each of these situations? You bet! Was I anxious? Definitely! However, it is the anxious people in this world who invent a better mousetrap, and that's what I did. As a result of the anxiety and pressures of being unemployed so frequently, I developed a system to get a job quickly; in fact, in thirty days. It became my personal system for more than ten years. Occasionally, I shared it with a curious friend or acquaintance. Eventually, I took the system and wrote the book *Get the Job You Want in Thirty Days*. In this instance, fear helped me figure out a better way of doing things. It helped me to work faster, smarter, and more effectively than the competition. This utilization of fear is normal.

Dr. Joyce Brothers, in her book, *Positive Plus*, eloquently explains abnormal utilization of fear as "a minefield of disasters." She explains, "There are many people whose anxieties are far from the norm." In these individuals, fear becomes an obsession. People become preoccupied with the fear of failure, question their ability to measure up to others' expectations, and they fear rejection. In cases like these, fear becomes destructive instead of constructive.

You can readily identify this type of fear. This obsessive fear interferes with the ability to concentrate. An individual becomes ineffectual at setting goals, working toward them, and striving until they are completed. In this type of fear, an individual is depleted of the vitality necessary to achieve success. In essence, paralysis by fear becomes a self-fulfilling prophecy.

Being out of a job and the resulting loss of self-esteem often bring out anxieties that are unproductive and result in depression and insecurity. Think of Tom, for instance, who was in the job market because his spouse's career moved them from New York to Florida. For many months he tried to keep his old job and commute to his new home on weekends. This was placing stress not only on his relationship but his finances as well. He knew eventually he would have to live in Florida full time and look for a new job. Tom admits he prolonged the inevitable. "What took more than nine months could have been considerably less if I had realized it was fear and low self-esteem that prevented me from taking action. Realizing what paralyzed me would have made the transition a lot less painful." Once Tom had diagnosed the fear factor, he quit his job, looked for another position, and was hired at a new company with a greater salary within a month of leaving New York.

HOW SEVERE ARE YOUR FEARS AFFECTING YOUR JOB SEARCH?

Check yes or no to the following questions.

	YES	NO
1. Have you experienced an unusual amount of irritability and anger when interacting with loved ones or friends while job hunting?	_____	_____

	Yes	No

2. Is there a noticeable lack of interest in work-related and even leisure activities you once enjoyed? _____ _____

3. Do you find yourself unmotivated, inactive, and lethargic for many of your waking hours? _____ _____

4. Have you experienced the inability to network and meet people because you are shielding yourself from rejection by remaining isolated? _____ _____

5. Have your fears prevented you from keeping to your daily goals and completing them? _____ _____

6. Are you afraid to share your fears, worries, and anxieties with a loved one, counselor, or friend? _____ _____

If you answered yes to any of the above questions, then your fears could be inhibiting your job hunt's success. In fact, your fears could be setting you on a course of self-fulfilling prophecy contributing to that which you fear most—rejection and defeat.

All is not lost. There is hope. In *Positive Plus* Dr. Joyce Brothers states, "The way to start dispelling your anxieties and bolstering your self-confidence is to diagnose exactly what that 'something' that you should do something about is. Once you pinpoint the source of your anxieties you are halfway to mastering your negative stress." Recognizing your fears is the first step to overcoming them. By addressing instead of avoiding them, you'll tame the psychological lions and tigers within by putting each fear into perspective.

Start out by making a list of the fears and anxieties you feel you need to tackle first. Review the ten most common fears cited by job hunters and career changers, which I have documented through my research. After reading the list, reflect a moment and diagnose any fears you may personally have that may not be included. By reading this list and adding your own, you will bring your fears out into the light, and by doing so, you will take control and master them.

THE JOB HUNTERS' TOP TEN FEARS

- I won't be hired because I'm overqualified.
- I'll never find a job I really like.
- My spouse will leave me if I'm unemployed.
- My kids will think I'm a failure.
- Others will think less of me.
- All I'll get is rejection for my efforts.
- I dread getting a job offer and starting over.
- I'm going to retire old, homeless, and poor.
- I won't be able to sell myself.
- My skills are outdated.

List any additional fears you may have.

- _____

- _____

- _____

- _____

- _____

Before we face each of the fears listed, we need to eliminate some of them. It has been said that nearly all of our worries and unhappiness are imagined and not actually real. After you read over the list a second time, you may discover that some of them may be extremely unlikely. If this is the case, cross them off now.

Dale Carnegie agrees with this tactic. In his book, *How to Stop Worrying and Start Living*, his Rule #3 states, "Let's examine the record. Let's ask ourselves: What are the chances, according to the law of averages, that this event I am worrying about will ever occur?"

In *How to Stop Worrying and Start Living*, Clyde W. Maas of Saint Paul, Minnesota, shares a classic story to illustrate the point. "The United States Navy used the statistics of the law of averages to buck up the morale of their men. Sailors who were assigned to high-octane tankers were often worried stiff. They all believed that if a tanker loaded with high-octane gasoline was hit by a torpedo, it would explode so violently that it would blow everyone to kingdom come.

"But the United States Navy knew otherwise; so the Navy issued exact figures, showing that out of one hundred tankers hit by torpedoes, sixty stayed afloat; and of the forty that did sink, only five sank in less than ten minutes. That meant time to get off the ship. It also meant casualties were exceedingly small. Did this help morale? This knowledge of the law of averages wiped out my jitters. The whole crew felt better. We knew we had a chance; and that, by the law of averages, we probably would not be killed."

Before you prepare to address your real fears, relax. What are you really worrying about? Think it through and remember the law of averages and determine whether or not it is likely to happen.

After dismissing improbable and irrational fears, in the upcoming chapters we will face each of the top ten fears of job seekers and, to bolster our self-confidence, we will decide how to handle each if it did come true. By following this procedure both for the top ten fears and the list you have created, you will eliminate worry with a concrete and viable plan that, when acted upon, will create positive results. We will look at worst-case scenarios for each fear. You will have a chance to analyze your options and thereby give yourself a better sense of control over the situation. You will be forced to think each fear through and decide how you could prevent it from happening and how you would handle it if it ever came true.

The following chapters will teach you to make your fears work constructively for you. You will learn how to use fear as a strong motivator that will force you to take action. Douglas Hunt, M.D., in his book, *No More Fears*, explains further. "This means that, if we don't worry, the outcome could possibly go against us, and we may fail to get whatever it is we value. If we know we will succeed, we have a feeling of security and confidence. Not knowing for sure, we feel insecure and thus suffer anxiety, but the upshot is that we will probably end up working harder." Put your own fears into a constructive mode by working harder and getting results. Follow the procedures and exercises in each chapter as they are laid out. The result is that you will create the psychological tools to help you overcome fear and join the positive winners and thinkers in life. You will get and achieve whatever it is that you want.

FEAR #1:

I Won't Be Hired Because I'm Overqualified

Professionals with ten, fifteen, or twenty years of experience often feel their salary levels and career status will prevent them from landing a new job. Although willing to take a lateral or lower-paying position, they believe that interviewers are looking to hire talent right out of college. As a job candidate, you may naturally feel threatened by enthusiastic young professionals who aren't earning as much. You believe you are unable to compete. To some degree, your fear is founded. Let's face reality. Recent downsizing of companies after the boom of the '80s has released an unusually large number of highly paid professionals into the job market. Many of these individuals will face a carefully masked version of age discrimination from hiring managers and personnel departments. According to the law, age discrimination begins at forty. Many executives in their mid-forties or fifties have been accustomed to paychecks reaching and surpassing the six-figure range. Robert Bruce states in his book, *Executive Job Search Strategies*, "Typically an organization will lay off three executives and replace them with two junior people or graduates fresh out of college. Those two new people will be expected to work harder and produce more than the outgoing three had to in the last ten years." Bruce further makes the point that the problem is compounded "as a result of youthful Personnel Department representatives who interview older applicants. Perhaps unconsciously, these employer representatives view the applicants as parental figures and shy away from hiring them."

The way to combat this fear is not to sue every time you feel you have encountered age discrimination. In most cases an issue such as this is hard to prove. The odds are a long shot in your favor and will take a lot of time and money, not to mention the bad reputation you could develop within your community. It is best to move on to your own solutions, handling this fear effectively and landing the job you want. This is where your time is better spent.

Jo, a bank manager in Ohio since 1976, had worked her way up into senior management from the job of secretary that she took when she started with the bank in 1969. In the early 1990s, her bank ceased operations. She was suddenly out of a job with little warning. After a couple of years of applying to various firms in the area, she felt overqualified for many of the better positions she had applied for. She was getting very few interviews.

After reviewing her résumé, it was easy to see why she was not getting interviews. In fact, it was easy to see why she appeared overqualified. For instance, her résumé began in 1969, listing her first position at the bank as a secretary. Further, under education, she had listed her high school as well as the date of her graduation. After we reengineered her résumé, she immediately began to get interviews. Her career in management at the bank began in 1976. This is where her résumé began. It also made good sense because we were able to cut her résumé to one page with this approach. That was a good explanation for the cut years if the subject ever came up in an interview. Finally, we completely eliminated the dates of her education. There was no need to create an age image perception by assigning dates to education. Rather, we took the approach to list only the name of the school, city and state, and the degree awarded. It was amazing how a few key résumé changes brought one of her worst fears under control. She felt better equipped to sell herself, once she got the interview. The goal was getting a résumé that reduced the perception of age and overqualification so that it would prompt an interview.

It's important when addressing this fear that you come up with a game plan as to how you are going to handle the issue of overqualification across the board—in your résumé, cover letter, networking, and interviews. Since you know it is going to be an issue, be prepared for it. Those who deny the problem will have an ineffective approach to overcoming it throughout their job hunt.

Mike, a midlevel customer service manager for a New York–based airline, found his career blocked because of industry downsizing and turmoil. He decided to shed the label "airline employee" and transfer his skills to another industry. He was prepared to make some short-term sacrifices to get his foot in the door of a more stable industry. Soon, however, his worst fear was realized. When he applied for a lower-level job that paid less than he currently earned, the interviewer told him he was overqualified. Knowing this objection would come up in an interview, Mike had prepared a prerehearsed response that he had role-played with a friend. He told the interviewer, "I understand your concern. However, I'm confident that you'll find my abilities to be an asset in this position. And, should you want to promote internal talent in the future, I'll have proven myself and have the years of experience to assume more responsibility effectively. Please realize my objective isn't to be department manager at this time. I desire to join a leading company where I can grow and prove myself over time." His answer convinced the interviewer to hire him.

I have encountered many individuals, who fear they won't be hired because they are overqualified, make excuses for everything and anything. They will often dominate the discussions with negative thoughts of why any approach will never work. These are the individuals who say, "If I get a job . . ." The winners I have interacted with always say, "When I get a job..." Winners focus on solutions and not excuses. In the book, *The New Rules of the Job Search Game*, Jackie Larson and Cheri Comstock make a similar point. "I will not use the word 'but' in any conversation; for instance, I will never say, 'I want to find a job but...no one's hiring people like me." Instead, Larson and Comstock say, we must focus on the positive. "I am going to learn new ways of job searching and improve myself. I'm going to *make* it happen."

In order to make it happen, you need to have a plan. Determination is important, but it's not enough. Now we must lay out a structure, a plan that will help eliminate this fear. It is the same plan we will use in the consecutive chapters. Further, you can use it for any and all fears that may be hindering your job search. Here's the plan:

1. Write out on a clean sheet of paper the fear you may be feeling.
2. Write out answers to the following questions: Why do I think I have this fear? Where has it come from?
3. Write out the worst that would happen if this fear became a reality. What would you do to handle the situation? Dr. Joyce Brothers, in her book *Positive Plus*, calls this "the Worst-Case-Scenario for your worst anxiety. This will make you think about your options and give you a sense of control. It will force you to face it and think in concrete terms about what you can do to guard against its coming true and how you would handle it if it did."
4. Write out as many action-oriented solutions as you can think of that will prevent this fear from occurring.
5. The final step to the plan is simple. Take action. Just do it!

Now, go ahead and apply this plan to the fear we addressed in this chapter.

STEP

1

State the fear.

• I won't be hired because I'm overqualified.

STEP

2

Answer the questions:
Why do I think I have this fear?
Where has it come from?

- I've heard there's a glut of people my age in the job market.
- Everywhere you read that companies are cutting back.
- My friends tell me that companies prefer to hire young talent at less cost than someone like myself.
- My résumé is so extensive, it's a dead giveaway that they can't afford me.
- One look at me in an interview—well, it's hard to hide the years, if you know what I mean.
- I'll end up interviewing with someone younger than myself, I just know it. They'll think I want their job.

STEP

3

Describe the worst-case scenario. What is the worst that could happen?

- The interviewer will confront me and say, "You are overqualified," and I won't get the job.
- The interviewer will not confront me and I just won't ever hear back from them.
- I may have to generate more leads, contacts, and interviews than others who are not challenged with this problem.
- It will take longer for me to find a job.
- I may have to find a temporary job while I look for the job I really want.
- I will have to take a part-time job in order to pay the bills.

4

Write down action-oriented solutions that will help prevent this fear from occurring.

- Shorten my résumé. Get it down to one page by removing earlier dates and work history that may reveal my age.
- Remove dates from my education. Just list the degree, university, city, and state.
- Tone down recent work history in my résumé to reflect more average responsibilities when applying for a position less than my current title.
- Get around age discrimination and prepare the right image for the interview:

  For example:
  > Shed a few pounds. Look athletic, energetic, and fit.
  > Update your wardrobe for the interview. The suits, shirts, and ties from ten years ago could help reinforce your greatest fear.
  > Consider a hairstyle change.
  > Select hair color that looks natural.

- At home, role-play a well-rehearsed response to an interviewer who implies or says, "You're overqualified." Include the following facts about older candidates:

continued...

STEP

4

(continued)
Write down action-oriented solutions that will help prevent this fear from occurring.

They bring to the job superior judgment.

Their experience and acquired wisdom makes them more productive than others.

They are settled and less restless than younger candidates. This means stability and continuity of work performance.

Minimal training is required, resulting in minimal costs normally associated with a new hire.

They are a ready pool of talent when the company needs promotable individuals. They save the company recruitment costs.

• Practice, practice, practice in order to be confident, knowledgeable, desirable, and self-reliant.

STEP

5

Take action.

Follow your action steps as listed above. Begin to implement them now. Without implementation, without trying, you're not succeeding. Denis Waitley, the author of *The Psychology of Winning,* states, "Losers do what is quick and easy, whereas winners do what is difficult and necessary." Without acting upon your plans, your fear cannot be overcome. Just do it!

FEAR #2:

I'll Never Find a Job I Really Like

Many job seekers felt comfortable in their previous employment and did not want to leave it. They probably felt content because of a number of factors. Perhaps it was a short commute, the boss was reasonable to work with, longtime friendships with coworkers were established, there was the ability to be creative, hold flexible hours, be challenged, and genuinely enjoy the required job responsibilities. The idea of working for another company threatens this established comfort zone.

To illustrate this, you may remember the legacy of People Express Airlines. To his credit, Don Burr, the founder and CEO, created a unique and challenging environment for employees. Most of the 4,000 employees had developed high levels of love and dedication for their jobs and the company. They experienced a number of factors that developed this commitment. The company held cross-utilization in high regard. Employees experienced challenges ranging from being a reservation agent to working in marketing and running a baggage claim operation all within a normal month's work. Furthermore, the employees were not called agents but customer service managers, otherwise known as CSMs. They were also called *owners*. Because of company financed stock options, actually they were. This approach gave employees a sense of dignity, pride, and empowerment within their daily environment. They experienced a sense of being in control of their jobs and careers. It was sort of like working in Utopia. But not for long. Enthusiasm turned to pain and disappointment when the airline had financial difficulties and was absorbed by Continental Airlines. The mood prior to and during the takeover was grim. Those whose jobs were cut had the tremendous burden of not only finding a new job quickly, but realizing there would never be another environment to work in quite like People Express. For those who remained with Continental Airlines, the burden was assimilating into a company culture, in many respects quite opposite to People Express. I, like many others who have been in this type of situation where we've liked our jobs, remained in disbelief. Many of my colleagues were fooled into believing there was no life after the People Express experience. Possibly you have felt this way, too, after leaving a job and company you really liked.

After a rewarding employment situation such as this, people react in one of two ways. The first is to *compare* all future employment as inferior to the previous one, which had brought such great self-satisfaction and fulfillment. (As we will see later, this reaction is farthest from the truth, but nevertheless a valid feeling.) The second reaction is one of a wake-up call, a willingness to rise to the occasion, to become energized and enthusiastically challenged. After a short time of grieving, these individuals pick themselves up, dust themselves off, move on, and experiment with new industries and new career paths. In the latter case, along with experimentation may come paying one's dues, such as training in new skill areas and experiencing short-term loss for long-term gain. In the end, it's all worth it.

One manager from another airline that went out of business whom we'll call Barry, reacted in the first manner described above. His response is easy to identify and hopefully you are not like him. Two years after his job was terminated, his career was *still* floundering. He had drifted from one temporary job to another. When I saw him, he continued to describe what a perfect company and job he had lost. A sort of "those were the days" type of discussion. A wide range of emotions were detected in our discussion, ranging from bitterness and anger to sorrow and helplessness. Without putting this into proper perspective, his fear escalated to the point where he couldn't function at home or on the job. A few years after losing his job with the airline, he experienced a series of illnesses that reflected his mental state. He remained at home, grieving and angry, with injuries such as a broken leg and back problems. His fear was soothed temporarily with alcohol. He eventually sought professional psychological evaluation and rehabilitation. Now, almost ten years later, he remains immobilized by the fear and belief he will never find career happiness again.

There are countless stories of individuals who, as professionals in various industries, repackaged themselves, capitalized on their inherent skills, and overcame their anger and fears. For example, Anita, an individual I know from People Express, landed a position as a manager in charge of event and meeting planning for a major consulting firm in New York City. Another individual, Eric, was hired as a human resource executive for Hertz in the New York/New Jersey area. Yet another, John, became a midlevel manager for American Express Corporation in Fort Lauderdale, Florida. The list could go on and on. How did they do it? Why do some people succeed and others fail? How can you be assured that you will be among the winners?

First of all, let's get the facts straight. Hear it loud and clear: *There is life after your previous job.* Let me repeat that. *There is life after your previous job.* Instead of acting like an unemployed computer specialist, architect, manager, etc., believe you are first of all a human being. There is an increasing danger in the workforce today to identify with job titles rather than identifying with inherent skills. You are a human being first, your job title second. Focus on your skills. Focus on your humanity. Who are you?

What makes you good twenty-four hours a day, not just at work?

John Jamieson, a specialist in career development and life transition with a private practice in Fort Lauderdale, Florida, explains it this way: "I am who I am. But, I am not what I do. Although, what I do contributes to who I feel I am." Here he suggests beginning to identify with inherent skills that identify who you are. Are you intuitive, creative, a problem solver, and an initiator? Once you realize who you are, you will be happy anywhere you are using these inherent skills. John Jamieson coaches his clients to "discover who you are now." He explains, "Whether they face this issue now, during a layoff, or face it at the time of retirement, they are going to face it." In his practice he finds continuous evidence that most people make the huge mistake of using their work to escape knowing who they really are.

In essence, you must realize that happiness may not be finding your exact same job title. But, you will be happy when you match your inherent skills (who you are) to any industry or job. Remember our five-step formula for handling fear that we implemented in the previous chapter? With that same formula, let's put into proper perspective the fear we have addressed in this chapter.

STEP

1

State the fear.

• I'll never find another job I really like.

STEP

2

Answer the questions:
Why do I think I have this fear?
Where has it come from?

- I've made many close friends at work over the years. It just will never be the same again.
- I knew my job very well. It will be difficult learning a whole new company and position.
- Most companies don't even hire for this position. They tend to promote from within.
- I had this job for so many years, no one will be able to match the salary and benefits.
- It's not realistic to think I'll find another job this close to home. No matter how you look at it, I'm looking at a minimum one hour commute, each direction.
- After all the seniority I've gained, I don't think I will like working for a company where I'll be just one of the gang.

STEP

3

Describe the worst-case scenario. What is the worst that could happen?

- I may have to be a consultant and have the headache of starting and running my own business.
- I'll end up in a job that I really don't like, and I'll be miserable every day I go to work.
- I'll start a new job and, who knows, after a few weeks it may not be terribly exciting but it will be tolerable.
- To cut costs, I'll have to move in with the parents.
- I'll open a pizza shop.
- In a fit of depression, I'll sit at home doing crossword puzzles, soothing my ills with food and drink, and gain weight.

STEP

4

Write down action-oriented solutions that will help prevent this fear from occurring.

- Make a list of ten to twenty of your soft skills that can be utilized in any position, at home or at work, anytime and anywhere. Example: I like challenges, good phone manner, enjoy problem solving, creative, etc.
- Make a list of ten to twenty possible jobs/industries that would most benefit from your soft skills.
- Rewrite your résumé to reflect your soft skills more than your hard technical skills, thereby demonstrating your versatility and where you would be your happiest and most productive.
- Make a list of potential companies that suit you best, contact them for a hiring name and address, and send your résumé and cover letter.
- Only interview for jobs that you determine will best utilize your soft skills.
- Accept only job offers that you determine best fit your soft skills criteria.
- Be flexible on other issues such as location, type of company, and the job's technical responsibilities.

STEP

5

Take action.

Follow your action steps as listed above. Begin to implement them now. Without acting upon your plans, your fear cannot be overcome.

FEAR #3:

My Spouse Will Leave Me if I'm Unemployed

Your spouse may unknowingly be fueling this concern in one of two ways. The first is by asking questions and making statements about your situation. For instance, he or she may state, "How are we going to make the car and house payments?" or "We'll have to borrow money from my parents, and you know I hate doing that!" As innocent as the statements may be, your interpretation of them may include feelings of mistrust in your abilities, nagging, and intrusion. It is likely you are hearing a different message such as, "I doubt if you will be successful, and I'm going to leave you if you don't get a job and start making money soon." The second way your spouse may be fueling this concern is by nonaction. When a spouse becomes passive and unresponsive, your reaction to this behavior may include feelings of confusion and helplessness.

If your relationship has already been under stress, it is times like these, when you are unemployed and job hunting, that the interpersonal chemistry becomes even more fragile and vulnerable. It is here that a fear of abandonment and loss will appear and reappear at magnified levels. The fear of loss, whether it is our job or marriage, is the ultimate insecurity. Loss is a major underlying anxiety that weaves its way through our lives. Conversely, the ultimate security is employment and a stable relationship. Here you have value and self-worth. The fear that your spouse will leave you is sort of a double whammy. A major loss has already been suffered through a layoff or unemployment. Now, in a job seeker's mind, the final blow is yet to come: the loss of the marriage, the relationship. In essence, the job seeker is shell-shocked by the loss of a job and now fears the loss of a valued relationship as well.

According to psychological research, childhood experiences of loss and abandonment will replay themselves in our adult lives. We subconsciously carry childhood experiences of loss, such as the untimely death of a loved one or the collapse of a family business and the hardships that followed well into our adult experience. We now fear all experiences that indicate loss and try to shield ourselves from them. The tension between the times in the past get replayed in the present. Most individuals are not aware of their powerful connection and association with adult situations like the loss of a job. John Jamieson in his practice in Fort Lauderdale, Florida, discovered, "There is a strong correlation between what happens in childhood and how that resurfaces in times like the stressful moments of looking for a job and/or being unemployed."

In the marriage of Barbara and Herb, their relationship reached peak levels of stress when Herb was laid off after a longtime career as a police officer in the southern New Jersey area. Barbara, an administrative assistant for a local manufacturer, became the sole provider for the family. Herb, unable to get his job search in gear, became a homebound crossword puzzle escape artist.

After weeks of working all day and coming home to cook and clean at night, Barbara's team spirit quickly turned to anger. She decided to confront Herb. She said, "Starting tomorrow, I expect one new job lead and one task in the house completed each day."

At first Herb resented her confrontation. A few days later, he thanked her for getting him motivated, focused, and out of his comfort zone. Barbara clearly demonstrated anger, which Herb initially took issue with. The fact of the matter is, anger can be healthy if expressed constructively. If your spouse is angry, learn to detect what type of anger it is. Barbara's anger was healthy and constructive, and here's why. It was healthy because it was what she was feeling, and it activated Herb. It moved him out of his paralysis. Further, the anger was directed into a constructive action plan, "a project a day" as Barbara called it. Most importantly, the plan was achievable, focused, and time-limited. It had everything that smacked of achievability for him. As a result, he had a beginning sense of success. It was something to build on.

Anger only becomes destructive when communication is virtually nonexistent. Couples often avoid constructive confrontations in stressful times. What usually happens is, like a volcano, something is going to erupt in a violent way, and it usually does. This scenario definitely fuels the fear we are discussing in this chapter.

In *What Smart People Do When Losing Their Jobs*, Kathleen Riehle encourages you to "face your spouse's raw emotions and build a positive emotional framework for him or her." Help your spouse to realize that his or her feelings of doubt are not fact. You can help ease your spouse's fears by minimizing the situation, cutting back on the dramatics, and exhibiting positive and winning statements showing confidence in your capabilities and in the overall job search. Tell your spouse daily what *positive* actions you took to secure employment. Keep the communication flowing. Update your spouse continuously. Your job seeking activities, when communicated effectively and in a positive way, will dispel the fears and doubts he or she may be harboring. In times of anxiety and stress in a relationship, you should communicate more, not less. This is the time to actively stimulate your conversations with one another. Reach out, remain open, and allow yourself to be vulnerable. Maximize your sense of communication and connection. People forget in times of stress that thoughts are thoughts and not valid feelings. Without open, assertive (not aggressive) communication, thoughts that run rampant are misconstrued as reality. In actuality, it is simply fear talking. It is not reality. Communicate clearly your underlying value and importance to your partner. Do not be misguided by the erroneous belief that your partner is not really there for you more than he or she is there for what you do. When this is at risk, we tend to believe, "If I don't get the next big one, my partner will leave me!"

Let me emphasize a couple of last points before we embark on our five-step formula for handling fear. First, remember that no one likes a whiner. Whining is a way of saying to ourselves, "If anyone is going to beat me up, it's going to be me." Second, it's okay to vent, but being moody, angry, and uncommunicative feeds your spouse's fear. Mood is a great way to hide. It is not a valid way to feel. If someone is moody, that person is not really feeling. If anything he or she is camouflaging feelings.

1

State the fear.

- My spouse will leave me if I'm unemployed.

STEP

2

Answer the questions:
Why do I think I have this fear?
Where has it come from?

- My spouse keeps asking, "When are you going to find a job?"
- My spouse has been uncommunicative ever since my job search has taken longer than I thought it would.
- I've always been a good provider. I don't know why my spouse would want to stay with me now that I can't contribute anything to our lifestyle.
- We've already had to borrow money to pay the bills. This is not a good sign.
- The in-laws keep talking about how successful their other children have been.
- My spouse has been unusually angry over this whole thing.

STEP

3

Describe the worst-case scenario. What is the worst that could happen?

- Upon discovering that I'll never find a good job, my spouse will leave me.
- I'll end up moving out of the house and rooming with my brother or sister.
- I'll go on food stamps until I find a job and live in a cheaply furnished room for rent.
- My spouse will get everything I own, and I'll start over in life with nothing after the divorce is settled.
- My spouse won't leave me, but I'll be required to take over all the household responsibilities in order to earn my keep. I don't even know how to cook!
- I'll have to learn how to cook, clean, and not mix whites with darks when doing the family laundry. My self-esteem is going to take a beating.

STEP

4

Write down action-oriented solutions that will help prevent this fear from occurring.

- Keep the lines of communication open on a daily basis between myself and my spouse.
- Update my spouse frequently concerning the actions I am taking to find employment.
- Avoid overspending and frivolous purchases until I'm employed again.
- Give my spouse room to be angry. Get it out, talk it out, and realize it's okay to have these feelings.
- Get up early each day and make my job getting a job. My actions will speak louder than words.
- Get my spouse involved in the job search process. I can solicit help with cutting ads out of the newspaper, generating leads from professional directories, mailings, and role-plays before job interviews.
- Learn to accept criticism from my spouse.
- Become involved in daily household responsibilities. For example, I can do the laundry, cook as needed, clean, and do my part to make sure all the career and domestic responsibilities do not become the sole burden of my spouse.
- I will not be negative and whine. I will avoid using phrases in front of my spouse such as, *I can't, It's impossible,* or *It will never work.*
- I will exhibit a positive attitude, making reassuring statements that indicate I believe in myself such as, *I can, I will, I will make it happen,* and *It's just a matter of time and I guarantee I will find a good job.*

STEP

5

Take action.

Follow your action steps as listed above. Begin to implement them now. Without implementation, without trying, you're not succeeding. Act upon your plans and your fear will be overcome.

FEAR #4:

My Kids Will Think I'm a Failure

All parents desire their children's respect and feel they must project a confident image of being in control and a competent provider. Unfortunately, being unemployed and possibly sending the kids off to school while you're in a house robe or pajamas detracts from this desired image. You may feel uncomfortable about the children not seeing you dressed for success, having extra money to spend, or having a clear direction in life. When children are involved, what is best? How much information should be discussed with them when a parent is facing a major career change that threatens a family's security? Is it best for the parents to discuss the situation strictly among themselves, or should the children be included as well?

Joe, an Ohio resident, not too long ago was faced with the decision of whether or not to take the school board up on their offer for early retirement after being a high school principal for many years. With two teenagers still living at home, he and his wife Rosemary decided it would be best to involve the children in the decision-making process. After all, they concluded, it could influence what choice of colleges lie ahead upon high school graduation for both children. Rosemary recalls the situation. "When Joe knew that he could retire early and go out on his own into some type of consulting, we immediately considered the children. We decided it should not be hidden from them. I thought it would be a good idea to talk about it as a family before we reached a final decision. It was important to us how we were perceived by our children and to let them become part of the decision-making process. We wanted their input. And you know? They were honored by this. I think it will make them more responsible adults by observing how we communicate and make decisions."

David, a resident of New Hampshire, agrees that open communication with the children in these types of situations is imperative. David and his wife have three children who were ages nine, thirteen, and fifteen when he was faced with a major midlife career transition. David's career brought him from being a journalist for a daily newspaper to becoming editor of a business trade publication. As editor, he worked for a family-owned business. With little advancement potential and little control over his future, he decided to quit and look for something else. He recalls how he opened up communication with the family regarding his career change. "My wife and I sat down with the children and let them know my quitting was going to create a fair amount of uncertainty for all of us. I underscored that I did not intend to make a mistake. I asked, 'How does everyone feel about that?' Their immediate reaction was one of support. It created a team spirit and a sense that we are in this together. We did not look at whether I would be perceived as a failure. Failure, we decided would not be in our thinking, but we knew there would be sacrifices. We might have to make sacrifices along the way."

Children at almost any age are old enough to understand and be receptive to open and honest communication. One grade-school-age youngster, upon hearing her father lost his job, offered to sew, make, and sell gloves to help support the family. It's important that open communication takes place because some children may feel personally responsible when traumatic things happen. It's an awfully big burden for any youngster to carry. One way to get the discussion going is to tell them what happened at work to cause your current situation. Tell them the steps you are taking while they are at school in daily or weekly progress reports. Negotiate with them needed assistance and teamwork. For instance, the older children can help reduce household costs by working with the younger ones as sitters and providing child care in the summer months.

Although the children may not be able to afford their accustomed lifestyle for a few weeks or months, set aside quality time on weekends. Make this time a positive experience. Take a nature walk in the park, have a picnic, cook and bake together, do a craft, or play family games. Creative activities such as these may actually turn out to be more meaningful than spending money you may not have for more elaborate and expensive outings. Use your creativity, and your children will remember these as special and happy times.

One very important lesson that kids can learn in times like this is to understand that as a parent, you are not perfect. When they realize this, they'll understand that they don't have to be perfect all the time, either. This is a freeing realization that fosters risk-taking, creativity, and success. Many parents spend too much time trying to be perfect. Besides being impossible, this places a lot of additional stress on the unemployed parent.

With all that said, let's place this fear into proper perspective with our five-step formula for handling fear.

STEP

1

State the fear.

- My kids will think I'm a failure.

STEP

2

Answer the questions:
Why do I think I have this fear?
Where has it come from?

- The children always talk about their friends' families and all the nice things they have.
- I think the children will respect me less if I can't give them the quality of life their friends have.
- Showing my children that I am in control has always been important to me to maintain my authority in the family.
- I want to give my children more than what I got growing up. Now I feel incapable of delivering it.
- The children need a good role model in life. I just don't feel like I'm that person in my present situation. They look up to their Uncle Jack and Aunt Bette more than me.

STEP

3

Describe the worst-case scenario. What is the worst that could happen?

- We'll have to curtail family spending until I get a good job. That means no more new clothes and nice things for a while.
- The children will have to make sacrifices, chip in, and take on more family responsibilities.
- They'll talk back to me and not respect my authority because they are not getting in life what they once had.
- The children will become angry and unmanageable.
- They'll tell me they would rather live with Uncle Jack and Aunt Bette.
- I'll have to accept financial support from their grandparents to keep the lifestyle they are accustomed to.

STEP

4

Write down action-oriented solutions that will help prevent this fear from occurring.

- Have a preliminary discussion with your spouse. Arrive at the best way, time, and place to explain the situation to the children.
- Initiate open communication with the children individually or collectively, depending on the plan you and your spouse feel is best.
- Reassess your perception of failure. Think of it in terms of short-term sacrifices in exchange for long-term gain.
- Allow the children to share in the decision making, game plan, and sacrifices. It will assist them in becoming more responsible adults.
- Brainstorm a list of fun activities that are entertaining and will build healthy family relationships but won't put you in the poorhouse. For example:

  Take an afternoon hike in the park.
  Have a picnic in the country.
  Visit the library. Discover books and videos that
      you can take home for free.
  Learn to bake a loaf of bread or cookies together.
  Check out the newspaper's free community activities bulletin board.

continued...

STEP

4

(continued)
Write down action-oriented solutions that will help prevent this fear from occurring.

Do a craft together. Tie-dye old T-shirts. That's
always cool.
Pick your own farm-fresh fruits and vegetables.
Save money on your grocery bill while you are at
it. Check out the farm animals while you are
there.

• Make periodic checks of the children's feelings and
emotions. Ask them how they are doing with things.
Keep the communication flowing.

STEP

5

Take action.

Follow your action steps as listed above. Begin to implement them now. Without implementation, without trying, you're not succeeding.

FEAR #5:

Others Will Think Less of Me

Shame is the driving factor in this fear. Whether we realize it or not, most people feel shameful about job hunting and being unemployed. We wonder how we are perceived by others. After all, unemployment goes against the great American work ethic. Shame causes us to internalize our problem and try to prevent others from finding out our condition. We fear their perception of us. This in turn puts our job seeking activities in reverse. Getting a job is a numbers game. If we feel shameful and embarrassed to talk with others, then we're not making contacts and playing the numbers game.

Not having a job can be likened to those fearful dreams of appearing in public with no clothes on. Being unemployed or looking for a job is a very vulnerable time in one's life. Most unemployed professionals feel ashamed about having to hunt for a job at this point in their lives. According to the article, "*Shame,*" by Robert Karen, "Shame is an emotional experience that has until recently been so thoroughly neglected that it might be considered psychology's stepchild." The article continues to say that it has only been recently that "the master emotion, the unseen regulator of our entire affective life" has been recognized.

Bob, the director of marketing for a large hotel company in the northeast, at this very moment is about to be terminated as a result of major company cost-cutting downsizing effort. He worries about how he will be perceived by others once he is terminated. As he explains it, "It's the shame of it all, that I'm not the superman I once thought I was, to my family and friends. It's a wake-up call to face my own limitations and learn to tolerate them." He continues, "From my perspective, so much of who I am is tied into what I do and how much money I make. To have both of those taken away in one fell swoop, as it soon will be for me, it's devastating. I think the older you are, the greater the fear becomes."

Being unemployed reinforces childhood feelings that one doesn't fit. It reminds us of the times when we felt subhuman, like a jock in a homeroom of brains, or a brain in a gym class filled with jocks. As adults, one way we attempt to belong and minimize shame is by having a job we are proud of. As a child, we may have thought we were subhuman because we failed at sports or were chastised by a parent for a bad grade in school. As a result, when we failed, we felt ashamed. These experiences from childhood get stored in the body. They get replayed when we are adults in times when we feel we do not belong, like when we are unemployed.

"What does shame require?" the late Helen Block Lewis asked. (She is the first person to recognize shame and study it in a clinical setting.) "That you be a better person, and not be ugly, and not be stupid, and not have failed? The only thing that suits it at this moment is for you to be nonexistent. That's why people say I could crawl into a hole, I could sink through the floor, I would die. It's so acutely painful."

What steps does one take in order to overcome shame and put one's life and job search in high gear? Here are four simple steps that, when implemented, will give you power over this fear:

STEP #1: ACKNOWLEDGE

Keep in mind that because of shame, you may be hiding. In this step, your goal is to break through the membrane of denial and secrecy. Admitting to its presence is in and of itself a major breakthrough.

STEP #2: COME OUT OF HIDING

"To heal our toxic shame we must come out of hiding," encourages John Bradshaw in his New York Times best-seller, *Healing the Shame That Binds You*. He continues, "As long as our shame is hidden, there is nothing we can do about it." To come out of hiding, we must be willing to openly and honestly share our feelings with our family and close friends. When we begin to communicate with others, we open ourselves to verbalizing, identifying, and clarifying our feelings, problems, and concerns. In return, we allow others to connect with us, observe us objectively, and offer constructive and helpful feedback. Ultimately, we allow others to help us to the point of connecting us to the right networking and individuals that can help us get the job we so desperately want.

STEP #3: FORM A SOCIAL NETWORK

John Bradshaw recommends, "The best way [to overcome shame] is to find a nonshaming intimate social network. The operative word here is *intimate*." We are social beings. We cannot live a fulfilled existence without others. As humans, we have an innate desire to love and be loved. We can become effective in our job search only when we have established an intimate network of family and friends who support us and believe in us. Further, join a group of job seekers that meets monthly or weekly. One such group has existed in Princeton, New Jersey, for over ten years. The group, headed by Neils Olsen, calls itself Job Seekers. They meet weekly at a hall in the town's Episcopal church. On any given night, fifteen to thirty or more individuals gather to share concerns, worries, anger, and ultimately discover support and strategies to become winners in their job search. If a group like this does not exist in your area, why not start it yourself? Begin by meeting at someone's home, a church, or local restaurant for breakfast once a week. You'll be surprised at how effective a group like this can be to help members achieve their job quest goals.

STEP #4: REALIZE THAT CAREER TRANSITIONS ARE NORMAL

Realize it is perfectly normal to have periods of career transitions and unemployment in your life. The average American will experience five career changes in his or her lifetime. Being unemployed or looking for a job is not what it used to be twenty or forty years ago. These days, it is a normal fact of life as dictated by the current economy and industry trends.

Now that we understand more of the origins of the fear exposed in this chapter, we will continue with our five-step formula to overcome it.

STEP

1

State the fear.

- Others will think less of me.

STEP

2

Answer the questions:
Why do I think I have this fear?
Where has it come from?

- I may have to take a job with much less prestige and importance than the one I currently have.
- My new job will probably not have the income potential that I am used to.
- If I take a new job that is less than what I have now, I will no longer appear to be the superman or superwoman I once appeared to be to others.
- I'll have to curtail my spending patterns and will no longer be able to impress others with my wealth.
- My friends will be disappointed in me when I have to decline invitations for parties and vacations that I no longer can afford.

STEP

3

Describe the worst-case scenario. What is the worst that could happen?

- Maybe I'll have one or two friends left, or worse still, none.
- Every time others see me, they'll exhibit patronizing pity for me and avoid discussing my job situation.
- I'll become the laughingstock of the neighborhood when I end up taking any job to pay the bills.
- The only friend I'll have is my pet.
- While my friends are out at parties and taking vacations, I'll be sitting home watching late-night infomercials, alone.

STEP

4

Write down action-oriented solutions that will help prevent this fear from occurring.

- Don't hide any longer. Admit and accept the shame and anger you are feeling.
- Share your feelings with a family member or a close confidant.
- Make note of childhood experiences when you were chastised for being a failure and the shame you felt. Discuss with someone close to you how these experiences may be influencing your current feelings of failure and shame.
- Solicit support from family and friends. Ask for their understanding, suggestions, ideas, feedback, and most of all, their leads and contacts for potential employers.
- Join a job seeker's support group.
- Start a job seeker's support group if one does not exist in your area. Here's how to do it:

    Form a group by contacting friends who are in the same situation as you. Contact area clergy and counselors listed in the Yellow Pages. Let them know they are invited to send job seekers to the group you have formed.

    Open each meeting by introducing new members and giving a brief statement concerning their career and employment goals.

continued...

STEP

4

(continued)
Write down action-oriented solutions that will help prevent this fear from occurring.

Next, spend a moment to discuss a career self-help book, a chapter or two of which had been assigned at the previous meeting.

Invite counselors and professionals to come and address the group for thirty to sixty minutes as often as is possible.

End the meeting with discussions, reflections, ideas, feedback, and the mutual sharing of leads and contacts.

Practice and stage interview role-plays together.

STEP

5

Take action.

Follow your action steps as listed above. Begin to implement them now. Without acting upon your plans, the fear cannot be overcome.

FEAR #6:

All I'll Get Is Rejection for My Efforts

For most individuals, rejection is not something that is dealt with on a daily basis. Sure, we've all had an idea or proposal shot down by our company or boss, but this type of rejection is sporadic. Having a fear of rejection is common in individuals who just haven't had a lot of experience at it. Salespeople, in general, make better job seekers in this respect because their career literally hinges on achieving constant rejection to achieve success.

I often ask in my seminars, "How many here strictly rely on the Sunday help wanted ads for their job search leads?" Routinely, I calculate better than 90 percent answer yes to this question. Next, I refer them to two sections in my last book, *Get The Job You Want in Thirty Days*. Here the job seeker is instructed to place the job search on the fast track by exploring the hidden job market where, according to the U.S. Department of Labor, 85 percent of all jobs available exists. In order to do this, the job seeker must perform the activities of cold-calling and telemarketing. The vast majority of job seekers, from my experience, abhor even the thought of performing these activities. Why? Because cold-calling and telemarketing require making a large number of contacts, the vast majority of which result in rejection. However, the focus of the exercise is not on the rejection but upon finding that one company that will say yes. All it takes is one yes. Who cares about all the no's it took to get there?

In order to place this fear into proper perspective, we must be willing to reassess failure. Some view each negative response as one step closer to the fires of hell. Down, down, down, deeper they fall into disgrace and failure. Others have reassessed failure. It is a learning process. They believe they will get better the next time. They believe they are getting one step closer to success. Each is right. In order to win, you must reassess your perception of failure.

Thomas Edison was asked by a reporter how he felt about the 10,000 experiments it took to create the lightbulb. His response was, "I learned 10,000 ways how not to make a lightbulb." We, like Edison, need to realize that success is just on the other side of failure. The losers in life never get past no. The winners don't have the sense to give up. They just keep trying. The fact of the matter is that the more no's you get, the closer you are to a yes. If you are not getting no's, you're not getting any closer to a yes. Make a commitment today to increase the number of no's you are going to get in your job search. Now you are on the right track.

Many participants in my seminars keep wanting to draw the group back to discussions about the easy way out. They rationalize, "Well, if the Sunday help wanted ads only represent 15 percent of the job market, then how do you feel about using a placement agency (headhunters)?" These discussions frequently come up after we have spent an hour on cold-calling, telemarketing yourself, and reassessing failure. Even after all of this, there is still something in all of us that wants to avoid rejection and seek the easy way out. One therapist I spoke with feels that many job seekers do not want to take responsibility for their situation. They want to make it someone else's responsibility. The job seeker who is preoccupied with totally relying upon headhunters for his or her job search is a classical example of this. The behavior of depending on others for our career's success demonstrates how there is still the child in all of us who wants to flee responsibility and be parented.

Take the case of Jorgen Roed, founder and CEO of Scanticon International Hotel Conference Centers. He discovered that success is usually just on the other side of rejection and failure. In Denmark, when he was twenty-six years old, he applied for the position of CEO of a start-up operation in Copenhagen. After preliminary screening interviews, he received a phone call rejecting his application. His response, however, was anything but standard. He immediately drafted an overview business plan for the new operation, as if he had been selected as the new CEO. He sent it to the president of the parent company, Esselte, in Stockholm. He explained that since he was probably viewed as too young for the position and his application had been rejected, he wanted the parent company to freely use his newly devised overview business plan. After all, he explained, it would be of no use to him. He received an immediate phone call from the president of the parent company requesting to see him personally for a final interview. He got the job and developed it into a successful venture over seven years. Going beyond rejections even after all seemed to be lost landed him a long-term career.

In general, successful job seekers see rejection as a positive thing and therefore have the impetus to never give up. They realize that getting a job is purely a numbers game. Make enough contacts with some intelligent choices and actions along the way, and you have the ingredients for success.

Let's evaluate this chapter's fear by addressing it with the five-step formula we have been using.

STEP

1

State the fear.

- All I'll get is rejection for my efforts.

STEP

2

Answer the questions:
Why do I think I have this fear?
Where has it come from?

- The last time I looked for a job, all I ever heard was, "No, no, no." I'm lucky to have ever found the job I had.
- All my friends who are in the job market do nothing but complain about all the rejection letters they receive.
- At an interview, I am not good at answering surprise questions to a hiring manager's satisfaction. As a result, they always end up selecting someone else.
- I've already lost my job. Nothing else is going to go right, either. No one wants me.
- There are others out there who are more qualified than me. The competition is fierce.

STEP

3

Describe the worst-case scenario. What is the worst that could happen?

- Every job I apply for will end up with a letter of rejection.
- Every contact I make, the person will tell me they are not interested.
- Each company I apply to will have no need for my position.
- Each rejection I get will bring me one step closer to lifelong unemployment, poverty, and dependence on food stamps.
- The more rejection I get, the more depressed I'll become.
- After all the rejection of trying to find a job, I'll end up in therapy just to recover from all the psychological damage.

STEP

4

Write down action-oriented solutions that will help prevent this fear from occurring.

- Reassess failure and what it means to you. Realize that if you are not failing, you are not trying.
- Determine to become a winner by increasing the number of contacts, failures, and rejections in your job search.
- Listen to motivational audio cassettes. Ask your local library's librarian for assistance in checking out the tapes that are right for you.
- Check out a motivational video cassette from your local library and watch it as many times as you need until the concepts sink in.
- The next time someone rejects you, send them a thank-you letter and ask to be considered for the next position that becomes available.
- The next time someone rejects you after an interview or series of interviews, send the top manager or executive in charge a polite letter and action plan of how you would have handled the position if you would have been hired.
- Role-play at home with a family member or friend. Create a well-rehearsed response for the most common objections that an interviewer might have about you. Now you are rehearsed and prepared to handle objections glibly and professionally. With this technique, rejection can be minimized.

continued...

STEP

4

(continued)
Write down action-oriented solutions that will help prevent this fear from occurring.

- Whenever you experience rejection, reflect on what you could have done better through the hiring process. Learn something that you will do better or differently next time.
- When rejection comes your way, don't blame others. Take responsibility and learn from your mistakes. As long as you blame others, you will never get to the point of controlling your success.
- Read a book on failures who became successful. Read the biography of President Lincoln. A major bookstore's customer service department can assist you in locating the right books to read.

STEP

5

Take action.

Follow your action steps as listed above. Begin to implement them now.

FEAR #7:

I Dread Getting a Job Offer and Starting Over

Many people have the concern that no matter what job they ultimately find, it may not be the right one. They may worry about the length of the commute or whether they will like their boss, coworkers, and job responsibilities. Because of this, subconsciously they may dread the ultimate reality, a job offer. Essentially, fearing the very thing we want may prevent us from getting a job. Let's take a look at a few of the frequent anxieties we commonly have about starting a new job.

THE COMMUTE

Currently, due to downsizing, many professionals are finding themselves out of work after being employed for many years in the same community, where they have lived, worked, and raised their families. Now, all of a sudden, they find themselves unemployed. Although entrenched in the community due to home, schools, family, and friends, finding a new job in the same area is not likely. What is likely is that a new job, when found, will require a commute either by car or public transportation. The commute in many cases could exceed one hour in each direction.

Bill, after completing twenty years as an executive for a New Brunswick, New Jersey, automotive retailer, was caught in buyouts and mergers requiring that he look elsewhere for employment. In an area already plagued with corporate downsizing, he had to apply for positions as far away as Philadelphia, more than an hour's commute from his home. With elderly parents and family to consider, relocating closer to a better employment opportunity after living in the same community all his life was no option. As a result, his job search has been placed in slow motion. He has been courting a couple of companies in the Philadelphia area for almost a year. He is still unsettled and noncommittal when it comes to making the final leap into a new job and a commuting lifestyle.

THE NEW BOSS

We tend to look at the worst case when theorizing about a new boss. It's only natural. We tend to believe he or she will be a dictator, have no personality, be demanding, incompetent, cheap, arrogant, and humorless. Not much to look forward to in the scope of landing a new job. I remember one job I had where all the above came true. I had just arrived in New York City after residing in southern Florida for eight years. One of my first days at work, I stood in my boss's office, tanned, smiling, and saying, "Good morning." His response, in a grumpy old voice, was something to the effect, "Go ahead, smile and laugh, because after a few months of living and working here, you'll be just like me, just like the rest of us!" Quickly, I responded, "If that happens, just take me out back like an old injured horse and shoot me." He barked a command, I left the office, and knew I was in for the time of my life. In hindsight, certainly not in a good sense, it was.

As a result of industry deregulation and reduced job security, I left that job almost two years later. What did I fear most about getting a new job? You guessed it. I was obsessed with what my new boss would be like. I was completely sure a new boss would come from the same mold as my previous one. In reality, it was farthest from the truth, yet the fear of starting a new job for this reason did control me to a large degree.

THE COWORKERS

If worrying about a new boss becomes obsessive for many, so does integrating with a new group of peers. Like the boss, the fear of the unknown focuses on the negative. In our worst imagination, our peers will be gossips, back-stabbers, prima donnas, jealous, nasty, lazy, and sneaky.

Coworkers, whether we realize it or not, play a decisive role in the happiness of our jobs and our work environment. It is for this reason we consciously or unconsciously worry about their role at a prospective new place of employment. Our good or bad past experiences with coworkers will influence our future perceptions of prospective peers at our new job.

JOB RESPONSIBILITIES

You walk in to work, hang up your coat, turn the coffee on, and pick up where you left off yesterday. You've been doing the same routine for many years. You've come to expect it, sort of like brushing your teeth every morning. All of a sudden, years of routine are shattered after corporate cutbacks resulting in layoffs and your own unemployment have taken their toll. You may miss the predictability of the UPS chap who walked in at the same time every morning as you finished your daily report. The same suppliers have knocked on your door for years and have virtually become family. They've helped you make your most critical purchasing decisions.

The above scenarios demonstrate that we are not only creatures of habit but creatures that desire to maintain and protect our comfort zones. For these reasons, we have anxiety about starting a new job. Simple patterns and routines have not been established. The fear of the unknown, the unfamiliar, can overwhelm us. Our apprehension about landing a new job is further fueled by greater issues that challenge our comfort zones. Issues like new job training create fear in us. Learning new procedures, paperwork, and politics becomes a concern. We are hesitant about the initial classroom training that may be required. We feel pressured just thinking about cramming in new information, studying for and taking tests, as well as preparing group projects during training. Many unemployed people will not acquire the same job title and responsibilities that they had with their previous employer. We undoubtedly realize that along with a new job comes a period of time when we will feel disoriented and incompetent, and that will cut to the very core of our normal desire for an established comfort zone. For most people, just the thought of this can immobilize their efforts to locate and begin a new job.

IN GENERAL

A job offer means a number of unsettling realities feeding our fear of getting the very thing we desire. It means back to set hours, learning a new position, the uncertainty of the unknown, bosses, deadlines—well, you've got the picture. We may rationalize that being unemployed, despite its hardships, is not a bad deal. It allows for flexible hours, time to be at home, and relief from the stress of a job. Often, job seekers have subconscious mixed emotions about giving this all up. The reality is, starting over can be exciting and positive. Instead of fear, we ought to focus on the new friends we will meet, the new training and skills we will acquire, and the money and recognition that we will get. This is the greater reality.

Let's explore how to overcome this fear further as we apply our chapter-by-chapter formula for overcoming fears and generating success.

STEP

1

State the fear.

• I dread getting a job offer and having to start over.

STEP

2

Answer the questions:
Why do I think I have this fear?
Where has it come from?

- It's the age-old adage, "You can't teach an old dog new tricks." I'm getting too old to be starting over.
- I dread starting over, only to discover after a few weeks or months it's not working out.
- I like staying home, watching TV talk shows, and enjoying my personal time.
- With my luck, I'll end up with the boss from hell. My life will be miserable.
- They'll require knowledge of computers and computer software programs. At my last job I got by without knowing about computers.
- I'm really not up for learning office politics. It took me too many years to learn how to work with everyone at my last job.

STEP

3

Describe the worst-case scenario. What is the worst that could happen?

- The company will put me through eight weeks of rigorous training. The learning curve will be so great all the circuits in my brain will be on overload. I'll end up on Prozac.
- Pleasing a difficult boss will become so frustrating I'll just completely lose it one day in front of the whole office staff.
- The commute will be so long I'll have to pack breakfast and dinner just to make it through the day.
- I'll miss out on all the daytime TV action and personal playtime.
- None of my coworkers will like me because they'll realize I think they are a bunch of scheming, two-timing gossips.
- After a few weeks or months it won't work out. I'll quit.

STEP

4

Write down action-oriented solutions that will help prevent this fear from occurring.

- Focus on the positive aspects of starting a new job. There are good things to recognize about the whole event.
- Realize you just might make some new lifelong friends.
- Accept that you will learn new skills that will expand your résumé and make you more valuable in the workforce.
- Envision the training you will receive as a way to save the cost of having to go to school to take the computer classes yourself.
- Realize there is a new generation of bosses out there who are consultative and trained to ask your opinion. You more than likely will get this type of person as your boss.
- Practice positive self-talk when you think of landing your new job.
- Envision the recognition you will get from family and friends when you land the job you want.
- Focus your mind on the fact that you will begin to enjoy a regular paycheck again.
- Write out a list of things you want to do for yourself and your family financially after the first few paychecks have arrived.

STEP

5

Take action.

Follow your action steps listed above. Begin to implement them now.

FEAR #8:

I'm Going to Retire Old, Homeless, and Poor

Tom Jackson, the author of *The Perfect Resume*, states, "This fear is imbedded in our culture from the Great Depression. It is imbedded in us from our parents." No matter how much we have or don't have, we still possess this fear. Even the rich have it.

My parents may be like yours. From early adulthood to this very day, they desire assurance from each of their children that they have job security, are paying into Social Security, and are paying monthly into a retirement account. They use the above-stated fear to motivate. I often hear statements like, "You better be putting your money away, or you're going to retire without a pot to do it in!" or, "I don't know why you work for that company. You better find a job with a better future." Many parents have raised their children with a mind-set to work forty hours a week for forty years for the same company, and Social Security will take care of you. My father, possibly like yours, did work for the same company for forty years. He retired with the achievement of having never missed a day's work in forty years. It was a different work climate and corporate culture after the war.

Today, it is nearly impossible in this economy to ever work for the same company for ten years, let alone forty. The rules have changed. Companies are trimming, computerizing, and modifying their labor forces to remain competitive in a global economy. This reengineering is the future we have to look forward to. The only constant that we are assured of is change. As a result, we need to break out of a different era's mind-set. More than likely, we will not retire at age sixty-five. With breakthroughs in medicine, people are living longer and more productive lives. Social Security will probably not be sufficient to take care of us. Many people, however, will remain productive doing a variety of things to maintain their income and remain valuable contributors to society. We need to rethink how much of the above-stated fear has been brainwashed into us by our parents, who lived during the Great Depression. Ever since then, we have been fed this rhetoric over and over.

In order to put this fear into proper perspective, we need to deprogram ourselves out of the mentality that you sacrifice yourself until the end and you'll get your just reward. Actually, according to most medical research done on retirees, those who retire with no purpose get sick and die earlier than those who emerge from retirement with a new career and purpose in life. The ones who continue to work in some shape or form remain healthy and vibrant. We need to realize that the only social security the future holds for our generation is the security we commit to providing for ourselves.

For hundreds of years, work has gotten a bum rap. Since, and even before the Industrial Revolution, workers were required to put in long hours in fields and factories. In more recent times, retirement has come to symbolize the antithesis of this struggle to survive. It promises an ideal life of leisure where there are few pressures and responsibilities.

The rules of work have changed, and so, too, have the rules of retirement. Researchers have delved into the retirement patterns of individuals in the last third of their life to discover that many of them choose to continue to work. More than likely you will generate income in your golden years by combining what you are really good at with what makes you happiest.

David Brown, producer of such hit movies as *Jaws, The Sting, Cocoon,* and *The Player,* has written a straightforward book on retirement titled, *Brown's Guide to Growing Gray.* In their book, *Beating the Age Game,* Jack and Phoebe Ballard combine their research on current retirement trends with David Brown's sometimes humorous insights. Brown quotes the famous literary agent, Irving Lazar, who at age eighty woke up one morning and had this to say: "If I didn't have something to do today, I'd rather be dead." Brown continues, "If you don't have something to do today, you *are* dead. You are not only dead but are also in a purgatory of boredom. Nobody needs you. No matter how your bones creak or what difficulty you have getting out of bed, I recommend that you *work yourself to death. It's the only way to live.*" Later, Brown declares flatly, "Almost everybody I know who feels young, vital and sexy—no matter what their age—is working." He recounts that George Burns booked to play London's Palladium when he turned one hundred. After all, George Burns quipped, "How can I die when I'm booked?" Although he never did play the Palladium, he had the right idea!

If that doesn't convince you that it is unlikely that you will retire poor, consider this. According to the U.S. Census Bureau, only 6 percent of married couples aged sixty-five and older have incomes below the poverty line. According to the results of the 1994 Retirement Confidence Survey, conducted by the Employee Benefit Research Institute (EBRI) and Matthew Greenwald and Associates, Inc., two-thirds of Americans believe that they will achieve financial security in retirement. The public at large is generally optimistic about their retirement. These statistics alone prove that we often do a whole lot of worrying about nothing. Dale Carnegie, in his book *How to Stop Worrying and Start Living,* states that over 90 percent of our fears never come to pass and are unfounded.

Let's further take control of this fear by implementing our established steps to overcoming it.

STEP

1

State the fear.

- If I don't land a great job, I'll retire old, homeless, and poor.

STEP

2

Answer the questions:
Why do I think I have this fear?
Where has it come from?

- I look at others around me, and they're doing very well for themselves.
- With all the credit card, house, and car payments I have, I've got to be just months away from financial collapse.
- I doubt my own abilities to pick myself up and keep going if my whole life collapses as a result of being unemployed. I'll give up.
- My parents keep telling me I'm going to retire old, homeless, and poor if I don't find a job soon. I've heard it so much I'm starting to believe it.
- My father had a great career with the same company all his life. I can't seem to compete with that in this day and age.

STEP

3

Describe the worst-case scenario. What is the worst that could happen?

- At age sixty-five, all I'll have is an $800 Social Security check to apply toward my monthly expenses.
- Upon retirement, I'll have to move in with one of my children or a friend.
- I'll have to keep working beyond retirement age in order to meet expenses and maintain the lifestyle I am accustomed to.
- When I grow old, I'll be in a homeless shelter working in a soup kitchen.
- I'll have to rely on the generosity of family and friends to supplement my income and take care of me. It will be a real blow to my ego.

STEP

4

Write down action-oriented solutions that will help prevent this fear from occurring.

- Block out negative self-talk like "I can't" with winning statements such as "I can. I always achieve what I set out to do."
- Deprogram yourself of the rhetoric regarding retirement that you were raised with. Replace it with an updated version where you are in charge of your retirement income not solely Social Security and a pension.
- Create new retirement goals for yourself. Decide what types of money-making ventures will motivate you and keep you happy in your golden years.
- Prepare now to have the health you need to accomplish your retirement money-making goals.
- Begin today to practice proper exercise, nutrition, and preventive medical exams that will help guarantee you a long, happy, and productive life.
- Stop comparing yourself with your parents, brothers, sisters, and friends. Accept who you are and what you have and will achieve in life.
- Talk your feelings over with a spouse or understanding family member or friend. They will have a more objective view of your skills and talents.

continued...

Step

4

(continued)
Write down action-oriented solutions that will help prevent this fear from occurring.

- On a piece of paper or in your own mind, strike a balance between what is a realistic fear and what is greed. A desire for a stable retirement is one thing. Obsessing over a fear that has excess and greed at its root is compulsive, unhealthy, and will never be satisfied, no matter what you do in life.
- Realize that statistically, you have a 94 percent chance of retiring comfortably. If you're willing to play the lottery, then this statistic should put a real smile on your face.

STEP

5

Take action.

Follow your action steps as listed above. Begin to implement them now. Without implementation, without trying, you're not succeeding. Denis Waitley the author of *The Psychology of Winning*, states, "Losers do what is quick and easy, whereas winners do what is difficult and necessary." Without acting upon your plans, the fear cannot be overcome. Just do it!

FEAR #9:

I Won't Be Able to Sell Myself

This fear becomes more intense the longer an individual has remained at the same company or in the same position. Self-selling skills are usually not a part of most people's job descriptions. Each person is good at what it is he or she does best. Most people have never given a thought as to how they would package their years of experience, communicate it, and sell it to another company or for that matter, repackage their skills for a totally different career path.

Ken, a marketing director for an international hotel company, found it difficult to toot his own horn upon learning his company would be downsizing. Much of his inability to apply his own marketing strategies to himself, he believes, came from a religious belief that to be humble is not to talk about oneself. He relates, "I find it difficult to sell myself. I was raised in a home where you do not give glory to anyone except God. My father always taught, 'To God be the glory.' You have this programming from childhood where you have learned that it is not nice to brag. It is very difficult to overcome. It is a real distortion of what it is to be humble."

Another reason most people feel uncomfortable selling themselves is performance anxiety. If I say I am superman or superwoman, then I am going to have to do it. I realize that if I put it out there, then I am going to have to make it happen. This sort of thinking leaves many people uncomfortable when it comes to the delivery of the goods. Most find it much safer to lower the ceiling, so to speak; this way it has that much less farther to go when it falls upon them.

After holding his previous job as an analyst for Symedco of Plainsboro, New Jersey, for almost four years, Jonathan was a victim of a classic case of downsizing. He observed how many people in his company when laid off, were in shock, paralyzed and embarrassed about losing their jobs. He was determined to be different. How did he do it? In one word, *selling*. He explains, "I began by selling myself on the telephone. When a call came in or I made a call, I had to sound like Wally on *Leave It to Beaver.* I did not speak or sound based on how I felt but on what the caller wanted to hear, someone energetic and enthusiastic about himself." Through his whole job search, he initiated a wide range of selling skills. His determination to sell ultimately produced an offer to take the position of indirect cost analyst at Princeton University.

This story should not be unusual, but it is. Most individuals have a fundamental aversion to anything that sounds like enthusiastic selling. It creates hesitation and fear in most people. But no matter how you describe it, getting a job is purely a selling situation and you are the product. Martin Yates, author of the career best-seller, *Knock 'Em Dead,* agrees: "Operating in a seller's market requires knowing who, where, and what your buyers are in the market for, then being ready with a properly packaged product." After all, you are the greatest product you will ever sell.

Most people feel they are not natural-born salespersons. They often make statements like, "I'm just not a salesperson by nature." Tom Hopkins, in his book, *How to Master the Art of Selling,* agrees with the premise that "everything about selling is learned." He also states, "Stop excusing yourself from the hard work of learning how to sell. It doesn't matter whether you think you're a wonder or a non-wonder, you still have to pay the learning price." This is good news. Effective selling skills are learned, not inborn.

When we talk about selling yourself, there are five main components of the job search process that you must learn in order to wisely and professionally implement your selling skills. They are:

1. The résumé
2. The cover letter
3. Generating leads
4. Interviews
5. Follow-up

Taking a look at each one of these components, we will identify which selling skills should be utilized in each step. We will discover ways to practically implement the required selling techniques and how to make each an effective step in the sales process.

THE RÉSUMÉ

The purpose of a résumé is to sell the interview, not to get a job. Individuals often try too hard to pack volumes of information into a two-, three-, and even four-page résumé. This common mistake is easily recognizable. The résumé appears cluttered, very little white space is apparent, and the typeface is small. Paragraphs ramble. What is wrong with this picture? Why is this not a good selling technique for a résumé?

In selling, rule number one is KISS or Keep It Simple, Salesperson. A reader cannot comprehend volumes of information, no matter how well your résumé is written, without having a face-to-face dialogue with you. Give just enough information to tease the reader and warrant an interview. This is the same technique advertisers use. An advertiser puts just enough punch in a thirty- or sixty-second broadcast to get you to come and see the product. Once they get you there, you are more likely to buy it.

You can achieve the desired sales punch in your résumé with the following tips:

- Top off your résumé with a bold headline, SUMMARY OF QUALIFICATIONS. Bullet four or five attention-getters about yourself that will appeal to the person who will read your résumé. Tailor these bullets to each company's needs. A computer is essential for this type of customization.
- Utilize action words. Stay away from cliché phrases. There is an exhaustive list of action words in *Get the Job You Want in Thirty Days* that will help you. A thesaurus is helpful, too. Remember, action words get attention.
- Keep it down to one page when answering ads or doing a mass mailing. Trust me on this. Keep the type size at twelve point, nothing smaller. Use bold caps for the résumé categories.

To sum it all up, in a sales teaser such as a résumé, less is better. Keep it short, make it visually appealing, and use action words to give it punch and command attention. The result: not a job offer, but you've sold the interview. Congratulations! That's all you want and need at this point in the sales process.

THE COVER LETTER

A cover letter is simply a sales and marketing letter. To be effective, the letter must follow proven marketing techniques. We can learn the correct techniques from the direct-mail letters we so frequently receive in the mail. Some we respond to, and some we don't. However, the fact remains: they work. What can we learn from these direct-mail marketing letters?

- It's a numbers game. The more letters you send out, the greater will be the response. Don't be satisfied with a three-, four-, or five-letter mailing. Plant a whole field of corn and you are bound to get results. Plant a few seeds and your risk of failure is greater. An effective mass mailing should be at least twenty-five to fifty letters.
- The first paragraph should get the reader's attention. In fact, coordinate the first paragraph with the four or five attention-getters in your résumé. Coordinating the attention-getters will leave the reader with a reinforced impression of your key selling features and how they will benefit the employer.
- The second paragraph correlates benefits to the company and the reader. Far too often, cover letters focus on facts but not benefits. Don't assume the reader will correlate the benefit. It's your job to correlate the benefit. For instance, say, "I have an M.B.A.," and the response is, "So What?" Add a benefit such as, "As a result of my M.B.A., I have learned high levels of critical thinking and problem solving that will enable me to get results under minimal supervision." Now, that gets attention.
- The last paragraph closes for the reader to take action. Most feel uncomfortable with this. Closing for action is a typical sales technique in letter writing and interviewing. Most letters I receive end with weak and begging pleas such as, "Hope to hear from you soon," or "I'll give you a call next week." This is not a close for action. A close for action asks the reader to do something. Just like the letters you get in the mail, "Call 1-800/ABC-XYZZ, NOW!" They ask you to do something. You must ask the reader to pick up the phone and call you at the end of your cover letter. Ask, "When can we arrange an interview? I may be reached at 213/484-6427." I like to think of the biblical expression, "If you don't ask, you won't receive."

Cover letters, like résumés, do not get jobs. The cover letter's sole purpose is to be a short three paragraphs that will sell the interview. The details of selling to get the job take place at the interview.

GENERATING LEADS

Bill was an unemployed engineer in Cleveland, Ohio, early on in the recent recession. After many months of answering help want-ed ads, his job search was going nowhere. He decided to get aggressive and fight back. Instead of relying on the help wanted ads, which only contain roughly 15 percent of all jobs available, he began to explore the hidden job market. He went to City Hall and retrieved the locations of businesses utilizing his background and skills. He began to go door to door, introducing himself to receptionists and anyone who would listen. After continuing this type of lead generation and self-selling activity, in less than two weeks he had two job offers. Both were unadvertised jobs where individuals had just quit and an urgent hiring need had been cre-ated. Bill's aggressive lead generation beyond the newspapers is where he found success. He took an offer from Iotech, located in Cleveland, near his home, where the president, Tom DeSantis, was impressed with his determination and strong will to win. Bill was offered the position of applications engineer and has since been promoted to regional sales engineer.

Bill's success formula is best described in an old sales term called *cold-calling.* In order to generate large amounts of leads through cold-calling, here are some tips to keep in mind.

- If you are unemployed, begin your day at 8 A.M. Get dressed in business attire as if you were going directly to work. By 9, arrive at an area where you can stop in on a number of com-panies that may hire for your type of position.
- Be prepared. In a black folder, carry copies of your résumé and a pen.
- Upon entering the office, introduce yourself to the recep-tionist and request to see the person in charge of hiring for your position. You'll be surprised; you will get interviews on the spot—up to five a week.
- If the person in charge is unable to see you, get his or her business card or a company card and write down the per-

son's name on it. Leave your résumé to be sent to that person.

• At the end of a typical day of cold-calling, you should have collected approximately fifteen to twenty business cards. That night, go home and send each person a cover letter and résumé.

With this activity alone, generating leads in a professional sales manner ends the concern, "if I get a job." With this type of daily activity it's not a matter of "if" but only of "when."

INTERVIEWS

The interview is the place where real face-to-face selling skills are necessary. Most job seekers, because they feel inadequate in these situations, experience enormous anxiety before and during an interview. What are the symptoms? We all know them: sleeplessness the night before, feelings of doubt while driving to the appointment, sweaty palms in the waiting area, as well as stuttering or stammering in the interview.

I recommend that those who have the fear of selling themselves at an interview should go on as many interviews as possible, whether they would like the job or not. The key is practice. Initially, try to get your first interviews with a company you would probably not work for. This is the time to make mistakes, get exposure to the process, and learn. After the interview, go home and make notes about your performance. How did you handle objections? Were you fluent and reasonable in your responses? Make corrections that you will implement at your next interview. Approximately five interviews later, you will be more than ready to zero in on interviews with your target companies.

With clear understanding and implementation of face-to-face selling skills, most of the unsettling symptoms described above can be brought under control. More importantly, utilization of effective selling techniques in the interview will make you appear desirable: confident, articulate, trustworthy, and a leader. Here are the key selling skills to keep in mind for an interview.

- Prepare, practice, and prepare. Effective selling begins the night before the interview. Role-play with a friend. Practice responding to the questions they will ask you. Rehearse well-thought-out answers to the difficult objections they are going to have about hiring you. Prepare your wardrobe, iron, polish, and get ready to shine with a winning image.
- Arrive at the interview early. If you arrive on time, you're late.
- Smile when you approach the hiring manager's assistant. Engage in a short icebreaker conversation. An article in the December 1994 issue of *Personnel Journal* states, "You may want to give second thought to your treatment of the administrative assistant, he or she holds more power than you think. In a poll of 150 human resources and other executives, 60% said they considered their assistant's or secretary's opinion of a job candidate—no matter what level—to be important." This survey reinforces the fact that we are always selling.
- Engage the interviewer in a brief icebreaker such as a sincere compliment about the company or office facility. Others include name-dropping mutual contacts, always remembering to smile, and a brief statement about the weather or a nonbusiness-related issue such as a recent sporting event.
- Ask lots of intelligent questions. People who ask questions are perceived as more intelligent than those who don't.
- Welcome objections. Objections mean the interviewer is trying to picture you in the proposed position. Rejoice when you get an objection. In fact, say, "I'm glad you asked that." This type of response says a lot about your ability to handle conflict and problem-solve, critical skills for any new hire.

After the interview is nearly complete, don't forget to ask for the job. It sounds simple, but most people omit this step. When the interviewer asks, "Do you have any final questions?" respond with a definitive, "Yes. When do I start?" Depending on the situation, a more modest statement might be, "What's the next step in the hiring process, and when will I be invited back for the next interview?" Remember, sales are only made by those who ask. If you don't ask for the order, don't expect to get it. In sales terms, this final step is called the close for action.

FOLLOW-UP

Effective selling continues with relentless follow-up. Commonly, participants who attend my seminars ask, "How far is too far when it comes to follow-up? Is there a point where follow-up becomes a nuisance?" These seem to be tough questions, but I have a simple answer with a strong illustration to back it up. In the words of Winston Churchill, "Never, never, never give up." There can never be too much follow-up.

Success is usually just on the other side of failure. Take the case of a job I applied for a few years ago. The rejection letter came back that someone more suited for the position was selected. Instead of placing the letter in the circular file as we usually do, I sent a reply to the director of human resources. I thanked him for at least acknowledging my status in the employment process. I let him know that I was convinced that his company was the best place for my skills. I enclosed an expanded three-page résumé requesting that I be kept in mind for other positions that might become available. To make a long story short, I received a call within two days. I was working for the company within three weeks of replying to my own rejection letter. Strong follow-up, even after all seemed to be lost, landed me a long-term career with this company.

In general, good salespeople never give up. They realize that making the sale and in this case, getting a job, is purely a numbers game. Make enough contacts with some intelligent choices and actions along the way, and you have the ingredients for making the sale.

This chapter has probably inspired you to sharpen your professional selling techniques. It's never too late to make it happen. Visit your local library or bookstore and read books on selling. Indulge in personal growth by listening to self-improvement tapes like Brian Tracy's *The Science of Self-confidence* and *The Psychology of Selling*. You don't have to be a born salesperson. With a little effort, you can make yourself one.

Now let's take a look at our success formula for handling the fear addressed in this chapter.

STEP

1

State the fear.

- I won't be able to sell myself.

STEP

2

Answer the questions:
Why do I think I have this fear?
Where has it come from?

- It's not nice to brag. My parents taught me that a long time ago.
- I've never liked salespeople anyway. I don't like when I'm being sold. I'm not going to do it, either.
- Selling? What am I, a piece of meat? The whole idea of selling myself makes me feel cheap. I feel like I'm an item on a used car lot.
- I'm a firm believer that you don't have to sell. They have to learn to accept me and hire me for who I am.
- Selling means to lie about myself to others. That is unethical and I don't agree with doing it.

STEP

3

Describe the worst-case scenario. What is the worst that could happen?

- The competition will have sales skills and I won't.
- The competition will get the job over me as a result of their better sales skills.
- When I go to sell myself in the interview, I'll come off worse than an actor in a C-rated movie.
- It may take an extremely long time to find a job.
- I'll never get a job.

STEP

4

Write down action-oriented solutions that will help prevent this fear from occurring.

- Read a book on selling techniques.
- Attend a professional selling skills seminar. They are usually announced in the business section of the daily newspaper.
- Practice selling skills with someone who has experience in sales.
- Role-play selling yourself at the interview days before the actual interview.
- Reassess your attitude toward humility. Make sure it is not distorted.
- Reassess your attitude toward being able to deliver beyond what is expected. Raise the ceiling.
- Cold-call every day. Get out there, knock on doors, and introduce yourself to managers and other hiring decision makers.
- Have your résumé and cover letter evaluated by a sales and marketing professional (not a résumé writer). Make sure these two instruments sell according to the guidelines described in this chapter.
- A good salesperson follows up. Make your follow-up phone calls and visits as explained in this chapter.
- Reassess your attitude toward selling. As Tom Hopkins points out, it is a learned skill. Anyone can learn to sell.
- As you learn to sell, teach others to sell. The more you teach, the more you will understand, reinforce, and implement selling skills in your own style.

STEP

5

Take action.

Follow your action steps as listed above. Begin to implement them now. Without implementation, without trying, you're not succeeding.

FEAR #10:

My Skills Are Outdated

This fear could be a valid concern. If you have let your skills become outdated, then you know what the answer is: fix it. This can be done in a number of ways. I once traded with a friend to take computer lessons. In exchange, I helped paint their house. You can attend professional seminars, classes, and volunteer at a profit or nonprofit organization to develop the necessary skills.

Nancy was executive assistant to the president of a company located in Princeton, New Jersey, for more than eight years. When the company began to decrease its operations in the domestic market, her job security was threatened. She explains, "I started to look in the newspaper for a job. All the ads required knowledge of a new generation of computer programs. This technology had come out over the past couple of years, and I had not learned it yet. I had two choices. First, I could sit there and worry about what it would be like to go on an interview and say, 'No, I don't know that.' Second, I could get proactive and learn what I needed to learn." Nancy did the latter. Over a month's time, she read books, studied on a friend's computer on her lunch break, and enrolled in a seminar or two to brush up on the programs she felt she needed to learn in order to get a good job.

At first, Nancy admits she was fearful and apprehensive about updating her skills, but she says, "However, I must admit now in hindsight, learning is exciting. It felt great to be learning something new." Within fifteen days of completing her self-paced study program, she found her new job. Nancy now works as executive assistant to the president of Carter Products, a division of Carter-Wallace.

By increasing your skill level, you add more value to yourself as a product in the marketplace. Nancy felt she increased her market value as much as 100 percent. Why? Because without expanding her skills, she might have never gotten the job she really wanted.

I believe in lifelong learning. I hope you do, too. Being successful in today's job market starts with an attitude of being educable. No matter what you've done in the past, commit yourself to remaining current and avoiding complacency.

In a tough job market, it is important to your success that you do a skills assessment. Fill in the exercise on the next page by following the steps listed below.

1. Determine your natural strengths.
2. Inventory your learned strengths.
3. List your weaknesses.
4. Determine how you will eliminate each weakness.
5. State the time frame in which you will have the weakness under control.

I have provided a hypothetical example in each column. Follow its pattern and go ahead and complete the rest of the exercise based on your own self-assessment.

SKILLS ASSESSMENT EXERCISE

	NATURAL STRENGTHS	LEARNED STRENGTHS	WEAKNESSES	ELIMINATE WEAKNESS	TIME FRAME
1.	Good memory	Writing clearly	Lotus 123	Take a one day course. Read a Lotus book.	June 3rd June 30th
2.					
3.					
4.					
5.					
6.					
7.					
8.					
9.					
10.					

When you follow the time frames you've set in the above exercise, just think about the value you have added to your own worth in the job market today. Combined with your natural and learned strengths, you have the ability to not only get a job quickly but to get the job you really want and get paid well for doing it.

It is possible, however, that you may be harboring an irrational fear. After all, you weren't successful in your last job by accident. Keep in mind that individuals often doubt their current abilities when they are in a vulnerable situation such as being unemployed. All the self-doubt you experience about your skills may be a temporary misinterpretation of yourself rather than the truth. Feelings of inadequacy run rampant because you are in a temporary state where you feel downtrodden and beaten. This is a common phenomenon among great performers and artists, both current and past. Masters in their field often are plagued with feelings of inadequacy and continually driven to prove themselves. It is sort of a paradox. On the one hand you have already achieved many years of success in your field. This did not happen by accident. You acquired and exhibited the right skills for a long period of time. Yet, a sense of inferiority can overwhelm the unemployed. The very person that was skilled for many years now all of a sudden declares himself or herself "unskilled." Tom Jackson states, "This subterranean fear needs to be overcome by exhibiting full confidence in your inherent capabilities." Reread your list of natural and learned strengths. This list will give you a springboard for effective self-selling dialogue when networking and interviewing.

Now let's take a look at this final fear and put it into proper perspective via the formula we have been using throughout this book.

STEP

1

State the fear.

• My skills are outdated.

STEP

2

Answer the questions:
Why do I think I have this fear?
Where has it come from?

- Technology is moving so quickly, I never feel like I can keep up with all the changes.
- All the ads in the newspaper are requiring skills that I have not yet been trained for in order to interview for the job I really want.
- I've known my skills have been outdated for many years, but I've not had the time to do anything about it.
- You've heard the expression, "You can't teach an old dog new tricks." Well, that's me. I'm getting too old to be learning new ways of doing things.
- The younger people coming on the job in recent years have all the new, updated skills. I don't feel like I can compete with them.

STEP

3

Describe the worst-case scenario. What is the worst that could happen?

- I'll go on an interview and I won't get the job because my skills are outdated.
- I'll go on an interview and find out that, although my skills need updating, the new employer will provide the training.
- Over the next few weeks, I'll have to work evenings and weekends in a self-paced learning mode to begin to update my skills.
- As I implement self-paced learning, I'll miss out on my favorite TV programs and social activities. My life will become dull and boring.
- I'll collapse under the pressure of having to learn new skills, and I'll throw in the towel. I can always make pizzas at Uncle Harry's shop for a living.
- After the first interview, I may just discover that I'm not as bad off as I thought I was. I'll have spent all this time worrying to discover all I have to fear is fear itself.

STEP

4

Write down action-oriented solutions that will help prevent this fear from occurring.

- Fill out the Skills Assessment Exercise in this chapter.
- Read at least one book on each skill area you perceive to be a weakness.
- Attend a seminar, trade school, or college course that will provide you with professional instruction for the skills you need to improve.
- Volunteer a few hours a week at profit or nonprofit corporations. Arrange to work in an area where you will acquire the new skills you need for long-term career growth.
- Trade with a friend. Have your friend teach you a new skill that you need that he or she is proficient in. Then offer to help your friend with something in return.
- Reassess your fear. It may be irrational.
- Go out on an interview or two and sell around your perceived weaknesses. Get a better feel for how critical these skills actually are. It may be possible that you are making this out to be bigger than it really is.
- Look at the skills you currently have and think of ways you can transfer them to a new industry.
- Get rid of negative attitudes toward learning. Reassess your attitude toward learning.
- Adopt the policy of lifelong learning. Don't allow complacency to set in.

STEP

5

Take action.

Follow your action steps as listed above. Begin to implement them now. Without implementation, without trying, you're not succeeding.

Further Help

Throughout this book, I have stressed the importance of confronting your fears with a five-step formula for success. You can help yourself further by applying the same formula to the other fears you listed with the top ten fears in the exercise at the beginning of this book. When you recognize a fear, take out some notepaper and follow the format we utilized at the conclusion of each of this book's chapters. With it you can bring any fear into proper perspective and under better control.

You can achieve further growth through self-help methods. Go to the library and read at least a book a week that will help you with your job hunt. Stop in bookstores to browse, and buy and read books that will address key issues confronting you. Purchase or borrow self-improvement tapes such as *The Psychology of Winning*, by Denis Waitley, *The Science of Self Confidence*, by Brian Tracy, and *The Secrets of Power Negotiating*, by Roger Dawson. All the above-listed tapes can be ordered through Nightingale-Conant Corporation, 7300 North Lehigh Avenue, Chicago, IL. Phone for their self-improvement tape catalog at 800/323-5552.

Consider professional help as well. Check with area churches, synagogues, and recreational clubs for job search groups that may be meeting at their facilities to support and help one another. There are clergy and therapists in your community who you could contact for personalized direction and help.

Being fearful and anxious can also be heightened or minimized depending on your daily nutritional patterns. When we are anxious, it is precisely the time in our lives when good nutrition often gets put aside. Many people gravitate toward comfort foods such as items that are high in sugar, fat, and caffeine. All of these foods play havoc with our moods and emotions. You don't need a degree in biochemistry to control your diet and thus help control your moods. Here are some practical pointers that you may already know, but there is merit in reviewing them.

- Maintain even blood sugar and mood levels by eating healthy meals made up of complex carbohydrates. This includes low-sugar, whole-grain cereals for breakfast with multigrain breads, potatoes, and fruits for snacks, lunch, and dinner.
- Reduce or eliminate caffeine intake from beverages like sodas and coffee.
- Reduce or try to eliminate products made with chocolate ranging from candy bars to cakes and pies.
- Exercise three times a week for at least thirty to forty minutes. Include in your fitness repertoire fast walking, jogging, stair climbing and/or swimming to raise your heart rate and get oxygen-rich blood to your brain and vital organs. You will complete your workouts with an elevated mood and a natural high. This is extremely beneficial for overcoming anxious feelings, worry, and fear.
- Take a daily multivitamin supplement.
- Read a book on proper diet, nutrition, and exercise.

EXERCISE YOUR POSITIVE MENTAL MUSCLES

You never see the cameras in the loser's locker room. To gain the attention that you rightfully deserve from family, friends, and employers, begin by being determined to be a winner. Exercise your positive mental muscles of self-talk (internal chatter).

Replace negative self-talk with positive, winning statements. Then, go and make those statements to others. If you think it and say it, you will do it. Henry Ford once said, "If you think you can or you can't, you're probably right."

Bibliography

Ballard, Jack, and Phoebe Ballard. *Beating the Age Game*. New York, NY: Master Media Limited, 1993.

Bradshaw, John. *Healing the Shame That Binds You*. Houston, TX: Health Communications, Inc., 1988.

Brothers, Joyce. *Positive Plus*. New York: G. P. Putnam's Sons, 1994.

Bruce, Robert. *Executive Job Search Strategies*. Chicago: VGM Career Horizons, 1994.

Carnegie, Dale. *How to Stop Worrying and Start Living*. New York: Simon and Schuster, 1984.

Dawson, Roger. *The Secrets of Power Negotiating* (audio tape). Chicago: Nightingale-Conant Corporation.

Gerberg, Bob. *An Easier Way to Change Jobs*. Englewood, CO: Princeton/Masters Press, 1993.

Grappo, Gary Joseph. *Get the Job You Want in Thirty Days*. New York: Berkley, 1994.

Grappo, Gary Joseph, and Lewis, Adele. *How to Write Better Resumes*. New York: Barron's, 1993.

Hopkins, Tom. *How to Master the Art of Selling*. New York: Warner Books, 1984.

Hunt, Douglas, M.D. *No More Fears*. New York: Warner Books, 1988.

Jackson, Tom. *The Perfect Resume*. New York: Doubleday/Dell, 1990.

Karen, Robert. "Shame." *Atlantic Monthly* (February 1993).

Larson, Jackie, and Cheri Comstock. *The New Rules of the Job Search Game*. Holbrook, MA: Bob Adams, 1994.

Lindley, Mary, and Richard A. Wedemeyer. *In Transition*. New York: Harper Collins, 1991.

Personnel Journal (December 1994).

Riehle, Kathleen. *What Smart People Do When Losing Their Jobs*. New York, NY: John Wiley and Sons, 1991.

Seelye, Richard, and O. William Moody. *The Selling Starts When the Customer Says No*. Salem, MA: Probus Publishing Company, 1993.

Tracy, Brian. *The Psychology of Selling* (audio tape). Chicago: Nightingale-Conant Corporation.

———. *The Science of Self-Confidence* (audio tape). Chicago: Nightingale-Conant Corporation.

Waitley, Denis. *The Psychology of Winning*. New York: Berkley Books, 1986.

———. *The Psychology of Winning* (audio tape). Chicago: Nightingale-Conant Corporation.

Yates, Martin. *Knock 'Em Dead*. Holbrook, MA: Bob Adams, 1994.

About the Author

Gary Joseph Grappo is founder and former president of CareerEdge, leaders of career seminars for colleges and universities and job fairs nationwide. He is the author of *Get the Job You Want in Thirty Days*, contributing writer to *The Wall Street Journal's National Business Employment Weekly*, and coauthor of the career best-seller, *How to Write Better Resumes*. His newest book, *Old Game New Rules*, is forthcoming from Berkley Books. He has been a top-level human resources executive for various national and international corporations. Mr. Grappo resides in Fort Lauderdale, Florida, and is president and CEO of ASTEC International, Human Asset Technologies, Inc.

CORRESPOND WITH THE AUTHOR DIRECTLY

Mr. Grappo appreciates hearing from readers of his books and participants in his seminars. Write when you have an experience to share as a result of something you discovered in one of his books. Success stories based on the use of his concepts are always welcome. Also, to order quantities of his books or to reach the author for a speaking engagement, send E-mail to the following address: GJGJoseph@aol.com.